HEALTH AND DISEASE

Bronwen Murison

Macdonald Educational

How to use this book

First, look at the contents page opposite. Read the chapter list to see if it includes the subject you want. The list tells you what each page is about. You can then find the page with the information you need.

If you want to know about one particular thing, look it up in the index on page 31. For example, if you want to know about vitamins the index tells you that there is something about them on pages 12 and 13. The index also lists the pictures in the book.

When you read this book, you will find some unusual words. The glossary on page 30 explains what they mean.

Series Editor
Daphne Butler

Book Editor
Heather Powell

Production
Marguerite Fenn

Picture Research
Kathy Lockley

Factual Adviser
Geoff Watts

Reading Consultant
Amy Gibbs

Series Design
Robert Mathias/Anne Isseyegh

Book Design
Jerry Watkiss

Teacher Panel
Steve Harley, Ann Merriman

Illustrations
Kevin Ancient Front Cover,
Pages 11, 22, 27
Kevin Maddison Pages 7, 9
Kate Rogers Pages 14–15, 18–19, 24
Sylvia Tate Pages 12–13

Photographs
ASH: 21
Daily Telegraph Colour Library:
26–27, 29
Sally & Richard Greenhill: Cover, 10,
15, 23, 25
Rex Features: 17
Save the Children Fund: 14/Mike
Wells 28–29
Spectrum Colour Library: 12
ZEFA: 6, 16, 20–21, 26

CONTENTS

YOUR LIVING BODY

Doing and feeling

To hold this book and read these words you are using your hands, your eyes and your brain. Your body moves and feels all the time. How does it happen?

Inside your body is a strong frame of bones called the skeleton. This skeleton supports your body and helps to protect the organs inside. Over and between the bones stretch the muscles, like thick living elastic. The bones are linked by joints so that they can move easily when the muscle pulls them.

The nerves in your fingertips let you feel the softness and warmth of a kitten.

Whatever you're doing, muscles are hard at work. Tiny muscles in your face help you smile or speak and larger ones move your arms and legs. When you make a fist your arm gets harder as muscles clench up to do their work.

Your brain tells your body how to move. It does this by using your nerves, which are tiny threads of feeling running all over you under your skin. They spread out from the brain and spinal cord like the roots of a tree. There are two kinds of nerve. Some let your brain know what they sense – tasty food or wet feet, perhaps. Others take messages from your brain to tell your muscles to move, so you can eat up or fetch dry socks. Feeling and doing can happen very quickly. If you have ever burnt yourself you will know just how fast you jerked away from the heat!

Your brain sends a message through the nerves to the muscles telling them to move your arm.

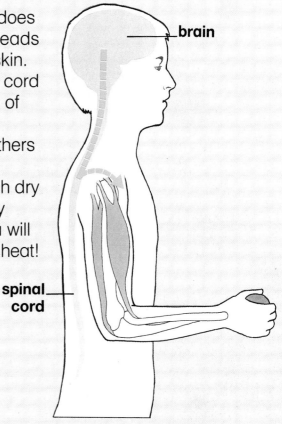

brain

spinal cord

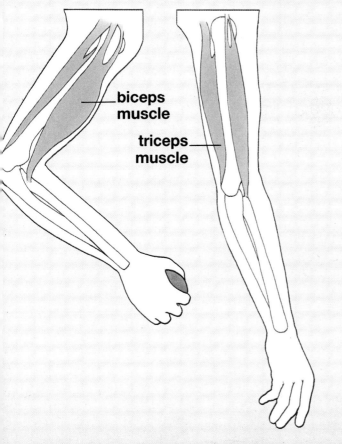

biceps muscle

triceps muscle

Your arm bends when your biceps muscle gets shorter and pulls your bone up. Your arm straightens when your triceps muscle gets shorter and pulls your bone down again.

7

What goes on inside?

Your body is working all the time, even when you are asleep. Your blood has to be pumped round your body and your lungs have to keep you breathing. Your body needs to grow and repair itself. You need energy to do these things and you need energy to be able to move around. People turn food into the energy they need to grow, to move and to stay alive.

When you swallow food it goes down a tube, called the oesophagus, into your stomach. In your stomach the food is churned into pulp. Then it is pushed down a very long tube, called the intestine. In the intestine the useful parts of the food, called nutrients, are taken into the bloodstream. Any parts of food that your body can't use carry on through the intestine. They are pushed out of the body at the anus.

Your heart pumps blood all around your body. The blood travels along many tubes called blood vessels. Some blood vessels are as thick or thicker than a pencil, others are as fine as cobwebs. If you look at your arms and hands you can see the blood vessels under your skin, they look blue. Blood takes the nutrients from food to the parts of the body that need them. Some nutrients provide energy; others are built up into muscle and bone. The blood also takes away things the body doesn't need, so they can be passed out of the body.

When you eat a banana it takes many hours for your body to get all the useful nutrients out of it. It can take 12 hours or more before the waste from the banana is pushed out at the anus.

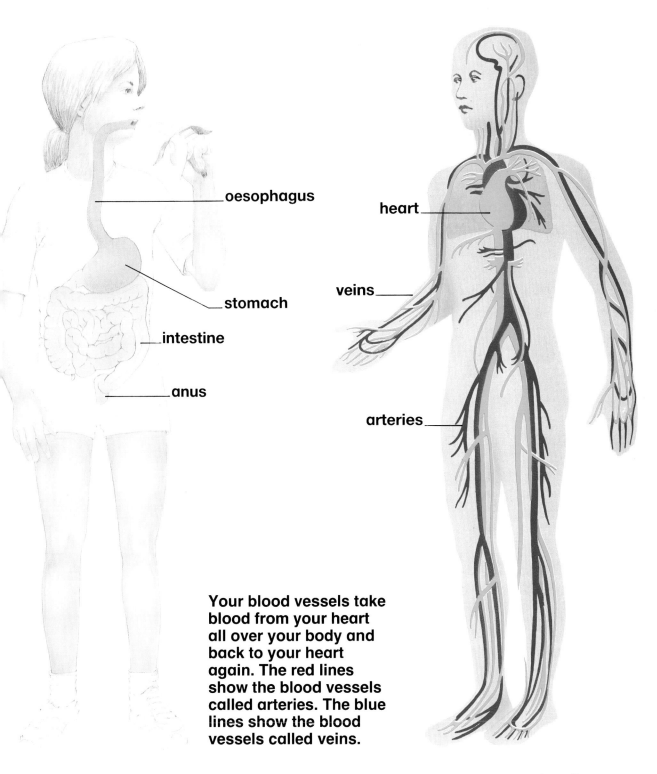

oesophagus

stomach

intestine

anus

heart

veins

arteries

Your blood vessels take blood from your heart all over your body and back to your heart again. The red lines show the blood vessels called arteries. The blue lines show the blood vessels called veins.

9

Living machine

Your body takes an important gas called oxygen out of the air to help turn food into energy. When you breathe in, you suck air into your lungs. Inside your lungs there are millions of tiny air sacs. These air sacs have very thin walls which contain very fine blood vessels. When the air reaches these sacs, the oxygen in the air can pass through the walls into the bloodstream. Then the bloodstream can take the oxygen round the body to help make energy.

Normally you don't think about how your body works and you don't have to tell your heart to keep pumping blood, or your lungs to keep on breathing. Your body won't let you stop living unless it is so badly damaged that it can't go on working.

Most children's bodies are fit and flexible because they are young and active. Older people who don't move around as much may need to do exercises to help keep their bodies supple.

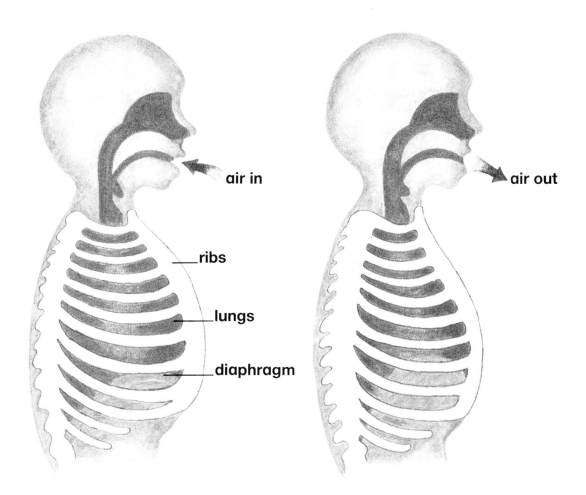

air in

ribs

lungs

diaphragm

air out

Your body can repair itself if the damage is not too serious. When you cut yourself, new skin will grow to heal the cut. If you break a bone, your body can mend it.

Your body should go on working for many years, but as you get older parts of it can wear out. Old peoples' joints can become stiff and their muscles weaker. When they get ill it's often because parts of them aren't working so well anymore. But whatever age you are, your body only works well if you look after it. You can help your body do its job properly by keeping fit and eating the right food.

When you breathe in deeply your muscles move your ribs out and your diaphragm moves down. This sucks air into your lungs. When you breathe out, your muscles relax and your diaphragm moves up. This squeezes used air out of your lungs. If you put your hands on your ribs you can feel them move when you take a deep breath.

KEEPING HEALTHY

The food you eat

The food you eat needs to have a mixture of seven important ingredients to keep you healthy. These are carbohydrates, fats, proteins, vitamins, minerals, fibre and water.

Most of the energy and warmth you get from food comes from carbohydrates and fats. You have a layer of fat under your skin to help stop your body losing heat. Fat protects delicate parts of your body, like your nerves. Protein helps your body to grow and repair itself.

There are many kinds of food. This market stall shows just a few of the different flavoured fruits and vegetables you can choose from.

Meat, fish and eggs contain protein. People who don't eat meat can get protein from beans and nuts. Protein is a body-building material.

You need tiny amounts of different minerals and vitamins to keep you well and make sure your body is working properly. The mineral calcium helps to build your bones and teeth.

Fibre is a part of food that cannot be broken down and taken into your blood. It travels down your intestine and helps to push waste out from your body. Cereals, wholemeal bread, fruit and vegetables contain fibre.

Water is very important because almost half your body is made from it. Your body can store food and use it later, but you lose water all the time you sweat, breathe or go to the lavatory. Most foods contain a lot of water.

Bread, potatoes, cereals and pasta contain carbohydrate, our main energy food.

Fats are found in butter, margarine, cooking oil and also in food like meat and cheese.

All fruit and vegetables contain some vitamins, minerals and fibre.

Minerals can be found in most foods. Foods made from milk contain calcium to give you strong bones and teeth.

Need and greed

Not everyone should eat the same amount of food: it depends on how much energy you need. An athlete has to eat more food for energy than a person who sits down in an office all day.

If you eat more than you need, the extra food is stored in your body in special fat cells. The more you eat, the bigger the fat cells get, and you put on weight. Too much fat is not good for your body. Fat can form on the inside of your arteries and stop your blood bringing enough oxygen and food to your heart. If your heart can't work properly you may have a heart attack.

Fresh fruit and raw vegetables make healthy break-time snacks.

Babies and children can't grow properly if they eat poor food. A balanced diet will help this baby grow stronger and healthier.

If you can't get enough to eat, any fat stored in your body is used up to keep you going. Gradually you become thinner and weaker. If you don't get enough protein, minerals and vitamins, you can't grow properly so your bones will be weak and bent. Your body can't repair itself either, and it isn't strong enough to fight against diseases. Very mild diseases that you cope with easily when you're healthy become much more serious and can even kill you.

Some people have too little to eat, and some people eat far more than they really need. To keep healthy you need a balanced diet: this is the right amount of food with the right mixture of ingredients.

Eating more than you need can be harmful, too. Overweight people can suffer from many health problems.

Keeping fit

Why do you do sports and PE at school? It's because exercise is good for your body. When you use your muscles by running, jumping and balancing they grow stronger. Strong muscles help you to do everyday things like climbing upstairs and walking to school more easily.

Some kinds of exercise help to strengthen your whole body. When you run fast and far, you use up more oxygen and you get out of breath. Your lungs work harder to bring oxygen into the blood and your heart works harder to pump the blood round your body. This extra work makes your heart and lung muscles stronger. If you keep fit you are less likely to suffer from heart disease or have a heart attack.

If you are ill in hospital and can't move much, you may be given a massage to exercise your muscles and keep them working.

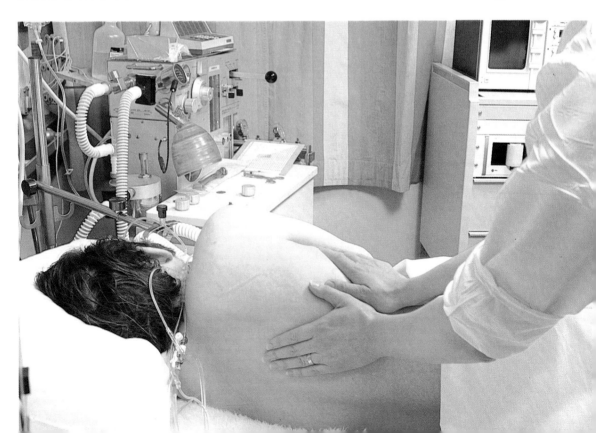

Any muscle which isn't used will become weak and flabby. People who can't walk or are ill in bed are given special exercises to do to keep their muscles working properly. Sometimes their muscles may be massaged because this will help to exercise them.

Staying fit is important for everyone. When your whole body is fit and strong it can stop you from becoming ill and help you to fight diseases. If you do get ill, or have to have an operation, you should recover faster if you were fit to start with. Regular exercise helps you feel healthy and stops you feeling stiff, weak and tired. Ice-skating, swimming, cycling or playing rounders are all good ways to enjoy exercise.

These marathon runners are being sponsored for each mile they run. They are using their health and strength to raise money to help starving people in other countries.

Healthy living

There are many things you can do to look after your health and help your body do its job. By going to the dentist regularly you can make sure that your teeth and gums are healthy. If there are any holes in your teeth, the dentist will fill them to stop them getting bigger. You can have your eyes checked when you visit the optician. The optician examines your eyes and tests them to find out how well you can see. You may need to wear glasses to help you see better.

Babies are taken to clinics where doctors and nurses can check their health. They are weighed and measured to find out if they are growing properly. Their ears and eyes are tested to make sure they can hear and see. They are also given injections to stop them getting diseases like measles.

Germs that feed on sugary food left in your mouth make an acid which eats holes in your teeth. You can protect your teeth by brushing them thoroughly every morning after breakfast and every evening before you go to bed, and by not eating sweets between meals.

The tiny water droplets you spread around you when you cough or sneeze are full of germs. It is important to cover your mouth when you cough and use a handkerchief when you sneeze so you don't spread your germs to other people.

Germs can grow in dirt, so keeping your house and your body clean helps to keep you healthy. It's especially important to keep the kitchen clean, because all your food is prepared there. Germs can be passed from dirty work surfaces and utensils on to the food you eat.

You use your hands for just about everything you do, and you can pick up dirt and germs from everything you touch. Make sure your hands are clean before you touch any food. If you handle food with dirty hands, the dirt and germs will be passed on to the food. The waste your intestine pushes out of your body has many germs in it, so you must wash your hands after you've been to the lavatory. These are very easy ways to protect your health.

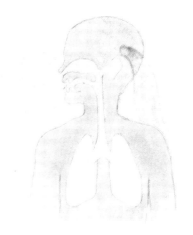

The germs in the water droplets get into the girl's body through her nose, throat and lungs.

19

How we live

The way we live can affect our health. More than a hundred years ago people didn't know how disease was spread, so they didn't worry about dirt. Rubbish was thrown in the street and left there because there were no rubbish collectors. There were only a few flushing lavatories and proper drains to take waste away cleanly. The water that was used for washing, cooking and drinking was often full of germs because no one knew it should be made clean before people could use it. Many people died from the germs which bred in the dirt around them.

Today we know much more about diseases and how to prevent them. Many people's lives are saved just because we have clean water, proper drains and our rubbish is taken away.

People's jobs can affect their health too. Miners' lungs can be harmed by the coal dust they breathe in while they are working. People who work with noisy equipment, like road drills, have to wear ear muffs to stop their ears from being damaged by the noise.

You can't always choose where you live or work, but you can avoid bad habits, like smoking. The tar in tobacco smoke damages the inside of your lungs and this stops them working properly. Smoking harms you and can harm people around you who breathe in your smoke.

This poster shows the tar from tobacco smoke that damages smokers' lungs. Posters like these are used to warn people of the harmful effects of smoking.

Germs will breed in rubbish which is left to pile up in the streets.

21

CURING DISEASE

Infections

You have germs in your body all the time, but most of them are harmless. When you catch a cold you are infected by cold germs which are attacking your body and making you ill. Harmful germs can get into your body through your nose, mouth or breaks in your skin.

Rotten food and dirty water can both carry germs and pass them on. You can spread infection to other people when you cough, spit, sneeze and even when you breathe. Insects like flies can pick up germs in rubbish dumps and other dirty places. When they land on food, they pass the germs on.

Your blood contains white blood cells which protect you against infection. When germs enter your body through a cut, the white cells destroy them. You can help prevent infection by making sure cuts are kept clean.

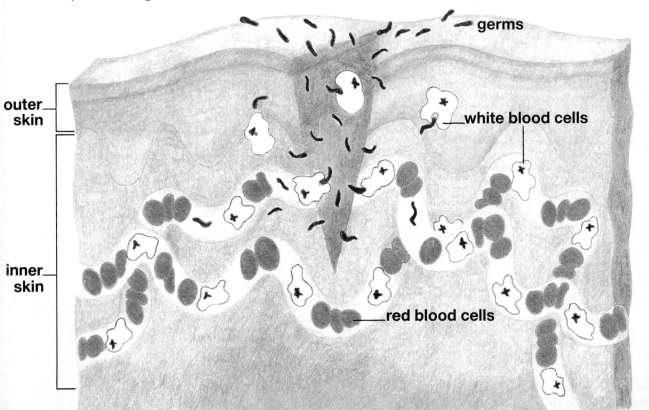

germs

outer skin

white blood cells

inner skin

red blood cells

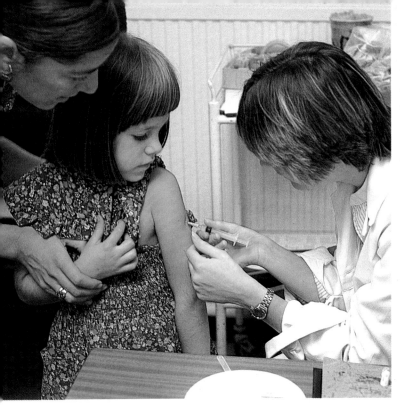

This child's mother has taken her to the doctor for vaccination. This injection will protect her from the diseases tetanus and diptheria.

Your body has ways of protecting you. Your eyelashes help stop dust and dirt getting into your eyes. The juices in your stomach kill many of the germs on food. Your skin is very good at keeping germs out, unless it is scratched or cut.

If germs do get into your body, you have white blood cells to fight them. Some germs can only make you ill once. Your body makes antibodies which will recognize those germs again and kill them before they have a chance to do any harm. You can make antibodies against some diseases, like polio, before you have ever caught them. A doctor can give you a vaccination which contains weak polio germs. This allows your body to make antibodies, but the germs aren't strong enough to make you ill.

Signs and symptoms

When you have chicken pox, everyone can see you are ill because you are covered with spots. The spots are a sign of your illness. If you have an earache, you are the only person who can feel that something is wrong. The pain you feel is a symptom of your illness. You can recognize a common illness like a cold from the signs and symptoms, but if you are not sure why you feel ill you should go and see a doctor.

The doctor will examine you to see if you have any signs of illness and you will have to say if you have any symptoms. Doctors and nurses are trained to recognize many different illnesses but sometimes they just can't tell what's wrong unless they look inside your body.

Nobody can see a headache but the pain this man feels is his body's way of telling him that something is wrong.

How can you tell that this baby is not well?

An X-ray machine will show your skeleton, so the doctor can see if any bones are broken. You can drink a special liquid which shows up on the X-ray to show whether there are any problems with your digestive system. The doctor can also use the X-ray to look at your lungs to make sure they are healthy. To get a clearer picture, the doctor may put a special fibre which acts like a telescope down your throat, or through your skin, to look at your body from the inside.

Sometimes samples of your blood or urine have to be sent away to a laboratory to be tested or examined under a microscope. All these tests can help the doctor find out what your illness is.

Healing people

There are many ways of helping ill people get better. Usually when you're ill you will visit your doctor. Your doctor might give you some medicine. There are many different kinds of medicine, but your doctor is trained to know which is the best one for curing your illness.

Some illnesses can be cured by an operation. Parts of your body, like your tonsils, make you ill if they get infected. If you are always having sore throats, your doctor might decide you need an operation to take your tonsils out.

Foods that are good for most people can make a few people ill. This is called an allergy. A change of diet can help cure some allergies. Children who are allergic to cow's milk must drink soya or goat's milk instead.

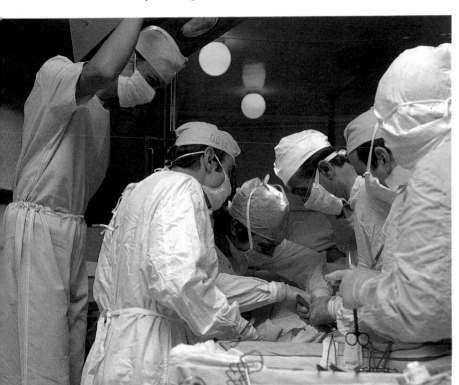

During an operation everything in the room must be clean and free of germs. The operating team cover their hands, faces, hair and bodies to protect the patient against infection.

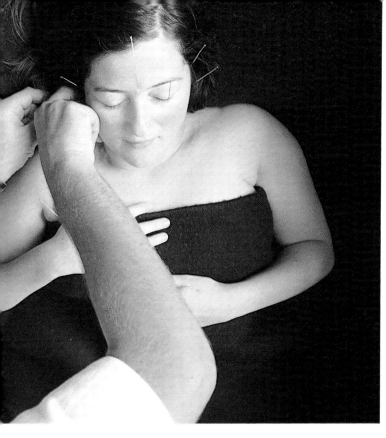

Acupuncture should not hurt, because the acupuncturist has learnt exactly where and how to put the needles in.

Healing may depend on very simple things. In some hot countries many babies get diarrhoea. They die because their bodies lose too much water. If water containing sugar and salt is dripped through a needle into a vein it replaces the lost fluid so the baby can recover.

Sometimes other ways are used to help cure sick people. In acupuncture fine needles are pushed into the skin in special places. Acupuncture can help to stop pain.

Herbs and plants have been used for many years to heal people. A herbalist knows what plants to use to cure illness. The plants are often made into a tea for the patient to drink.

Have you ever stopped a nettle sting hurting by rubbing it with a dock leaf?

All round the world

Some countries cannot afford to make sure that their people have the things they need to stay healthy. Because good health is so important, richer countries work together to try and help.

Money is needed to pay for medicine and hospitals, better drains and clean water supplies, and the training of doctors, nurses and other health workers. Doctors and nurses come from many different countries to use their skills and pass their knowledge on. Some countries train local people called barefoot doctors. They are taught how to treat some of the most common diseases. In large countries, doctors and nurses may have to travel long distances to reach as many people as possible.

At this clinic doctors examine children to make sure they are well and give them treatment for disease if they need it.

Posters are a good way of passing on information about health. This poster gives advice to parents of babies suffering from diarrhoea.

The care of children is very important. Clinics are set up to make sure that babies are getting enough to eat and are growing properly. They are vaccinated against diseases. Parents are taught how to give their family a balanced diet.

Growing enough food can sometimes be difficult. Crops can be killed by insects or drought, so farmers are taught ways of fighting these problems.

People living in hot countries around the equator have other problems to face. Germs can breed quickly in the hot, moist climate. Some diseases, like malaria, are caused by insects that only live in these areas. Scientists are working all the time to find ways to cure and prevent disease.

GLOSSARY, BOOKS TO READ

A glossary is a word list. This one explains unusual words that are used in this book.

Arteries Blood vessels that take blood from the heart, around the body.

Cells The smallest units of living material. Your whole body is made up of millions and millions of tiny cells.

Cereals These are any kind of grain, like wheat, rice or corn. Breakfast cereals are made from these grains.

Diaphragm A sheet of muscle attached to the lower ribs. Movement of the diaphragm helps suck air into the lungs.

Digestive system This takes nutrients and water out of food and passes the waste out of the body. The digestive system begins at the mouth and ends at the anus.

Drought A period when no rain falls for months. Water supplies get used up, no crops can grow, and animals are short of drinking water.

Equator The imaginary line around the middle of the earth which divides it into two equal parts. The equator is the same distance from the north and south poles.

Germs A word used to describe all sorts of minute living things which can cause illness.

Infection When germs get into your body and make you ill.

Laboratory A building or room where a scientist works with special equipment to carry out tests on materials like blood, or to do research into disease.

Massage Where a skilled person presses and rubs the patient's body with their hands. It takes away pain and stiffness from muscles and joints.

Microscope An instrument that makes very small near objects seem larger. It is used for examining objects that are too small to be seen clearly with the naked eye.

Operation Where the body is cut open in order to put right or remove a diseased part.

Organs Parts of your body with a special job like your heart or lungs.

Soya milk A drink made from the seeds of the soya bean plant. Soya beans contain protein.

Tonsils Small organs at the sides of the throat near the back of the tongue. Tonsils help trap and destroy germs. If they become infected you get a sore throat.

Veins Blood vessels that carry blood back to the heart.

BOOKS TO READ

The Doctor by Anne Stewart, Hamish Hamilton, 1985.
Feeding and Digestion by Dr Gwynne Vevers, The Bodley Head Ltd, 1984.
Moving by John Gaskin, Franklin Watts Ltd, 1984.
Just Look At Health by Brian Ward, Macdonald Educational, 1984.
The Heart by John Gaskin, Franklin Watts Ltd, 1985.
Teeth by John Gaskin, Franklin Watts Ltd, 1984.
Jimmy Goes to the Dentist by Barrie Wade, Hamish Hamilton, 1984.

Rudie Nudie

To Izzy, Charli, Cat and The Bundles

ABC
Books

The ABC 'Wave' device and the 'ABC For Kids' device are
trademarks of the Australian Broadcasting Corporation and are
used under licence by HarperCollins*Publishers* Australia.

First published in Australia in 2011
by HarperCollins*Publishers* Australia Pty Limited
ABN 36 009 913 517
harpercollins.com.au

HarperCollins*Publishers*
Level 13, 201 Elizabeth Street, Sydney, NSW 2000, Australia
31 View Road, Glenfield, Auckland 0627, New Zealand

National Library of Australia Cataloguing-in-Publication entry:

Quay, Emma.
    Rudie nudie / Emma Quay.
    ISBN: 978 0 7333 2335 5 (hbk.)
    For pre-school age.
    Australian Broadcasting Corporation.
A823.3

Designed and typeset by Ellie Exarchos
Emma Quay used pencil, paper
 and Photoshop for the illustrations
Colour reproduction by Graphic Print Group, Adelaide
Printed and bound in China by RR Donnelley on
 157gsm Chinese Gold Sun Matt Art

5 4 3   12 13 14

Rudie Nudie

story and pictures by

Emma Quay

ABC
Books

One, two Rudie Nudie,
    Rudie Nudie in the bath.

Squeaky clean and splishing, splashing, sploshing—

Rudie Nudie laugh.

Rudie Nudie
bye-bye bubbles.

Rudie Nudie dripping wet.

Dancing footprints on the bathmat,

Rudie Nudie pirouette.

Rudie hugged up in a bundle.
Rudie Nudie on the floor.

Rolling over,

jumping up,

and Rudie Nudie out the door.

Rudie all along the floorboards.

Rudie Nudie on the rug.

Tiptoe
quickstep
on the
doormat,

Rudie Nudie
nice and snug.

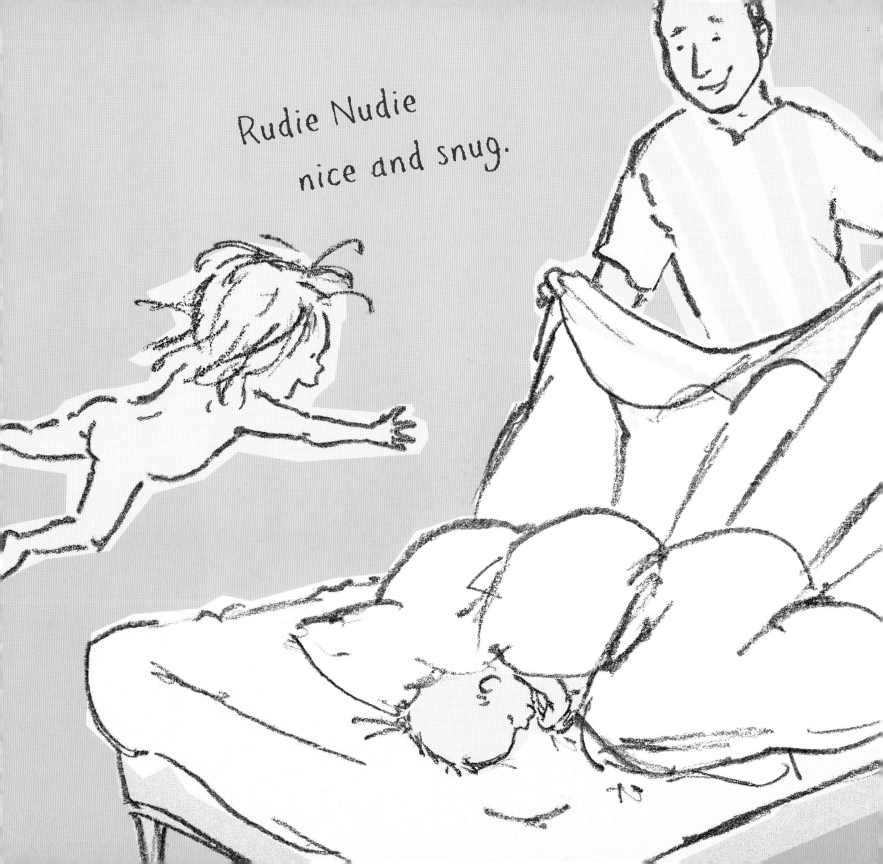

Rudie roly-poly tumbles.

Rudie Nudie circus clown.

Loop-the-loop until we're dizzy,

Rudie Nudie all fall down!

Rudie Nudie through the screen door—

Rudie running everywhere.
Rudie Nudie round the garden,

and a tickly under there!

Rudie Nudie, Mummy's calling,
'Rudie Nudie, getting cold?'

Rudie run up for a cuddle,
kiss and hug and squeeze and hold.

Rudie Nudie,
   pull on jarmies.

Rudie Nudie, time for bed.

But no longer Rudie Nudie—
no...

we're snuggled up instead!

Night, night.